HOW KATHERINE JOHNSON

A Computer

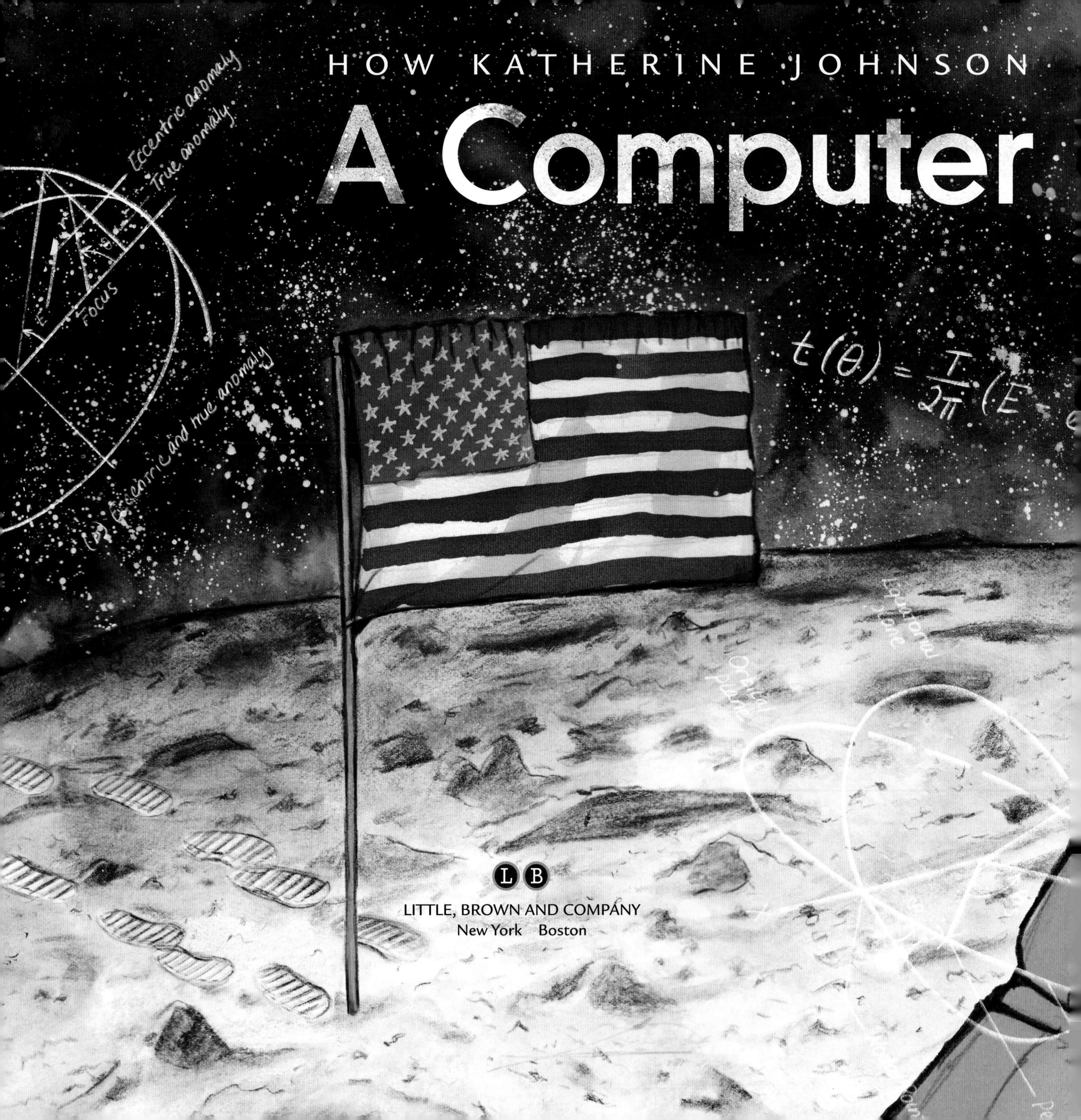

Eccentric anomaly

True anomaly

Focus

Eccentric and true anomaly

$t(\theta) = \frac{T}{2\pi}(E$

Orbital plane

Equatorial plane

L B

LITTLE, BROWN AND COMPANY

New York Boston

HELPED PUT AMERICA ON THE MOON

Called Katherine

Written by Suzanne Slade ✳ Illustrated by Veronica Miller Jamison

Everywhere she went, Katherine counted.

She counted her steps to church.

She counted the plates on the dinner table.

7
8
9
10!

She even tried counting
the stars in the sky.

Most important of all, Katherine counted the days until she could start school. Finally, at age five, she followed her brother (hundreds of steps!) to the two-room schoolhouse.

An excellent student, Katherine devoured thick books and added numbers at the speed of light, so the teacher decided she would skip first grade and start in second. But Katherine was such a fast learner, she later skipped fifth grade too. And before you could say "mathematician magician," **she was a grade ahead of her older brother!**

Katherine loved math because it was easy to see if an answer was right or wrong. Meanwhile, most everyone in town was arguing about "right" and "wrong." Some people said it was wrong for children with different skin colors to attend the same school.

Others said it wasn't right for women to work at the same jobs as men.

Their arguments seemed wrong to Katherine—as wrong as $5 + 5 = 12$. She believed everyone should be treated the same. So she kept working hard in school and dreamed of a future when all people would have equal rights.

Katherine finished eighth grade when she was only ten years old, but her town didn't have a high school for black students. Determined to keep learning, she counted the dusty miles— 120 in all—as her family moved closer to a school she could attend. There she took an exciting math class called geometry. She learned how points and lines made shapes—triangles, trapezoids, and perfect parallelograms.

$$a^2 + b^2 = c^2$$

$$A = bh$$

$$s = \theta r$$

$$V = \pi r^2 h$$

And her love for math grew exponentially!

At fifteen, Katherine started college. She flew through every math class at West Virginia State, so a professor taught harder classes just for her. In advanced geometry, she plotted points on a graph. When she connected the points, they created a beautiful U-shaped curve called a parabola. It was love at first sight!

After graduation, Katherine became a math teacher. Back then, people said women could only be teachers or nurses. Katherine knew that was wrong—as wrong as $10 - 5 = 3$. She believed women could be anything—scientists, lawyers, or mathematicians.

Katherine discovered a research center in Virginia that was hiring women mathematicians. They were called "computers" because they made calculations that helped the men engineers design airplanes and flight plans.

To Katherine, it added up to the perfect job!

All day long, she punched buttons on a calculator, just like the other women. She solved long math equations, just like the other women. She wrote answers on a huge data sheet, just like the other women.

But Katherine wasn't like the other women. She asked questions. Lots of questions! What were her calculations used for? Why were they important? How did her answers help design airplanes and flights?

The men engineers noticed the woman who asked intelligent questions and how quickly she solved difficult math problems. So they asked Katherine to join their space team. Its mission—send America's first astronaut into space.

Katherine said yes! Then she discovered that women weren't allowed to attend the group's meetings. She knew this was wrong—as wrong as $5 \times 5 = 20$. So she asked if she could go.

"Women don't ever go to those," the engineers replied.

"Is there a law against it?" Katherine asked.

"No."

So Katherine showed up at the next meeting—ready to work. Astounded by her geometry skills, the team asked her to calculate when America's first spaceflight should blast off. Katherine agreed. But first, she asked questions like:

Where should the rocket splashdown?

How high should it fly?

y

When should it land?

$(a) \sin \gamma = 2l$

$t(\theta)$

Eccentric anomaly

r

θ

Focus

anomaly

$e \, s$

With that information, Katherine carefully computed the rocket's flight path—a beautiful U-shaped curve! Next, she worked backward to figure out the time it should blast off.

Then she began counting the days until launch.

On May 5, 1961, Alan Shepard blasted off.

Following Katherine's flight path, he soared into the silvery sky.

Fifteen minutes later, he splashed down in the Atlantic Ocean—right on schedule.

And right on target!

Soon, Americans began dreaming of a longer flight—around the entire Earth. To figure out the math for this long, complicated trip, engineers decided to use their new, room-sized computer that worked much faster than people. But astronaut John Glenn trusted Katherine more than a machine. He wouldn't step one foot onto the rocket until she said the computer's calculations were correct. Happy to help, Katherine checked every number.

On February 20, 1962, John Glenn became
the first American to orbit Earth!

Then people began wondering if an astronaut could travel all the way to the *moon*. Both the Soviet Union and the United States wanted to be the first to land there and win the "space race."

Katherine knew this flight was incredibly long—and dangerous. Every calculation would have to be perfect. One math mistake and the rocket would zoom right past the moon!

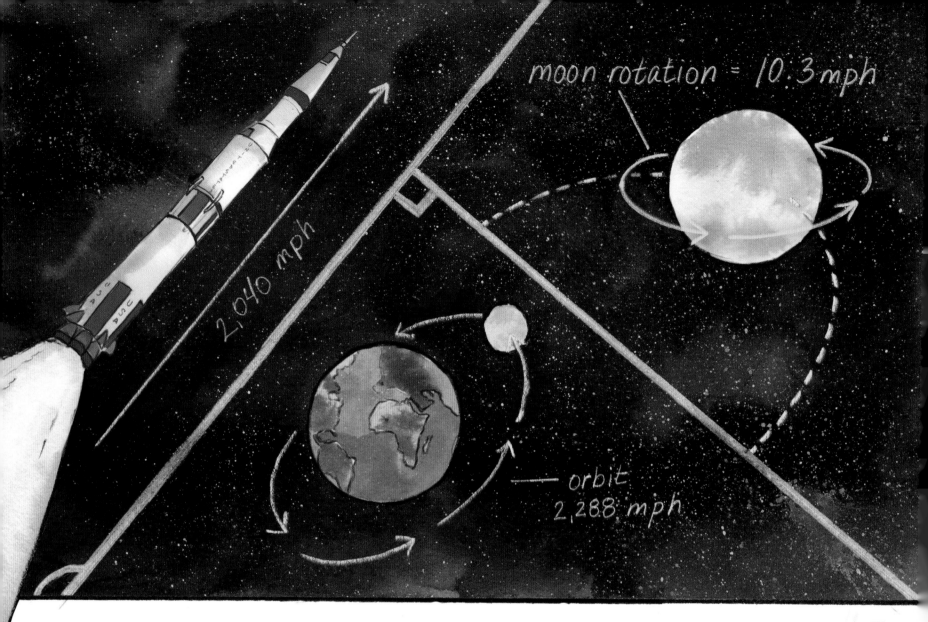

As NASA's computer hummed and computed a flight path to the moon and back,
Katherine went to work too, double-checking the machine's calculations.
But this was the most complicated geometry problem she'd ever seen.

One of the points—the spacecraft—was flying incredibly fast.

Her target—the moon—was constantly circling Earth (while spinning!).

Some people thought the problem was too difficult to solve. But
Katherine knew that was wrong—as wrong as 25 ÷ 5 = 4.

She calculated and computed.
She plotted and planned.
She created a bold, brave path all
the way to the moon—and back!

APOLLO
LUNAR LANDING MISSION

"Ten, nine, ignition sequence starts…"

Heart racing, Katherine leaned close to the small television screen.

"Seven, six, five…"

She held her breath as powerful flames exploded on the launchpad.

"Four, three, two, one…**LIFT-OFF!**"

The rumbling rocket slowly rose
above the ground,
above the smoke,
above the clouds,
and then disappeared into ink-black space.

Four days later,
as Neil Armstrong took
his first steps on the moon...

...Katherine smiled,
and began to count.

"Girls are capable of doing everything men are capable of doing." —KJ

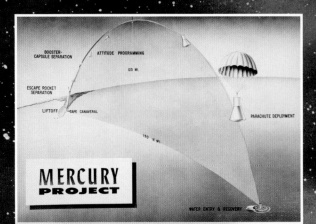

Proposed flight path for Alan Shepard's first American spaceflight

Katherine Johnson at her desk

NASA report co-authored by Katherine

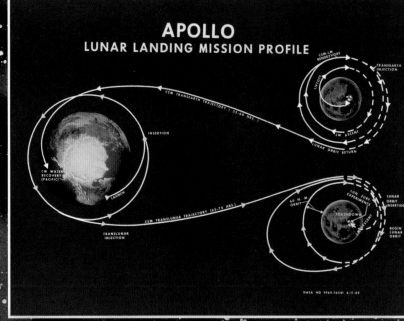

Apollo's proposed flight path to land on the moon and return to Earth

"If you want to know, ask a question. There's no such thing as a dumb question." —KJ

Time Line

1915: NACA (National Advisory Committee for Aeronautics) is created.

August 26, 1918: Katherine Coleman is born in White Sulphur Springs, West Virginia.

1928: Katherine starts West Virginia State High School at age ten.

1932: Katherine begins studying at West Virginia State College at age fifteen.

1937: Katherine graduates from college with a Bachelor of Science in Mathematics and French (summa cum laude) at age eighteen.

1939: Katherine marries James Francis Goble.

1953: Katherine begins working at NACA's Langley Aeronautical Laboratory (later known as Langley Research Center).

1956: Katherine's husband, James, dies of a brain tumor.

October 1, 1958: NACA becomes NASA (National Aeronautics and Space Administration).

1959: Katherine marries Lieutenant Colonel James Johnson.

May 5, 1961: Alan Shepard's spacecraft follows the flight trajectory Katherine helped plot, making him the first American in space.

February 20, 1962: John Glenn becomes the first American to orbit Earth after his spacecraft follows the trajectory verified by Katherine.

August 6, 1965: The Voting Rights Act of 1965 enforces voting rights for people of all races in all states.

July 16, 1969: Apollo 11 blasts off following the flight path designed and approved by Katherine.

July 20, 1969: Neil Armstrong is the first person to walk on the moon.

July 24, 1969: After following Katherine's flight path back to Earth, the Apollo 11 crew splashes down in the Pacific Ocean.

1973: Congress approves August 26 as Women's Equality Day (this is the day the Nineteenth Amendment—giving women the right to vote—was passed in 1920 and is also Katherine's birthday).

1986: Katherine retires after working for NASA for thirty-three years.

November 24, 2015: President Barack Obama awards Katherine the Presidential Medal of Freedom (the highest honor given to a civilian).

AUTHOR'S NOTE

When I first learned of Katherine Johnson, in November 2015, I immediately felt a connection with her because I also adored math from a very early age, pursued my passion for it in college, and later worked on rockets and spacecraft in the aerospace industry, surrounded by men. During my research for this book, I especially enjoyed listening to Katherine share her experiences in interviews, as well as researching photos and documents from her childhood and work at NASA. She is a true trailblazer for women in science and math, so I was pleased to see her story gain worldwide admiration through the *Hidden Figures* book and movie.

Katherine's love of numbers began at a very young age. As a child, "Katherine counted whatever crossed her path—dishes, steps, and stars in the nighttime sky." She became a "computer" in 1953 when she went to work as a mathematician at the National Advisory Committee for Aeronautics (NACA) in Virginia. NACA became NASA a few years later, in 1958. As a computer, Katherine calculated the flight trajectories and orbits for historic space missions and worked on the Space Shuttle program. She retired in 1986 after thirty-three dedicated years at NASA. In recognition of her valuable contributions to the space program, she has received honorary doctoral degrees and other awards. She even has an entire building at NASA named after her—the Katherine G. Johnson Computational Research Facility. On November 24, 2015, President Obama awarded Katherine Johnson the highest civilian award: the Presidential Medal of Freedom.

ARTIST'S NOTE

When I was asked to illustrate the story of Katherine Johnson—an American math and science treasure—for my debut picture book, I was thrilled! But I was even more excited to create art about a young black girl's love of learning. Can you imagine what it must have been like to have a mind filled with numerals, equations, and shapes, all swirling around like a vibrant dream? How exhilarating it must have been to dive into the mathematical theories of great thinkers past and present, and to use those ideas to launch humankind into the future?

While working on the illustrations, I connected deeply with Katherine's familial history and with the teachers and advocates who nourished and encouraged her gifts. When she was a child, schools were segregated, and black children often had fewer resources and lower-quality facilities. Katherine's own father was educated only through the sixth grade (much like my own grandfather, who made do with an eighth-grade education). And yet, so many black families like Katherine's (and mine) remained staunchly committed to getting their kids a better education and opportunities to thrive. Thanks in large part to her family and friends, we now celebrate Katherine Johnson as the genius mathematician who helped NASA accomplish many of its greatest achievements. I'm proud to have helped create this book about her for young readers, who I hope will be inspired to use math, science, words, and art to change the world themselves.

For my math mentor Judith Dalka, and to Ruth Spiro for her inspiration. And sincere thanks to Olivia McKee and Joyce Clemens, women "computers" at Langley. —SS

For the Millers, the O'Bannons, the Scotts, and the Jamisons. Especially for Callie Jhené. —VMJ

SOURCES AND CREDITS

Page 14 (Katherine and engineers' dialogue): MAKERS profile, Katherine G. Johnson, "Katherine Johnson, NASA Mathematician," http://www.makers.com/katherine-g-johnson.

Page 26 (countdown): Apollo 11 Flight Journal, "Launch," https://history.nasa.gov/afj/ap11fj/01launch.html.

Page 30 (quotations from Katherine): WHRO TV interview, *What Matters* segment, "Katherine Johnson: NASA Pioneer and 'Computer,'" https://www.youtube.com/watch?v=r8gJqKyIGhE.

Page 30 (diagrams, photograph, and report): Courtesy of NASA.

Page 32 (quotation): Margot Lee Shetterly, *Hidden Figures: The American Dream and the Untold Story of the Black Women Mathematicians Who Helped Win the Space Race* (New York: HarperCollins Publishers, 2016), 71.

The illustrations for this book were created with ink, watercolor, marker, and colored pencil on mixed-media paper. In some instances, no reference materials were available for details depicted in the illustrations, and the artist used the best sources available to represent those scenes. This book was edited by Deirdre Jones and designed by Saho Fujii. The production was supervised by Virginia Lawther, and the production editor was Jen Graham. The text was set in Legacy Sans, and the display type is DIN Schrift.

Text copyright © 2019 by Suzanne Slade · Illustrations copyright © 2019 by Veronica Miller Jamison · Cover illustration copyright © 2019 by Veronica Miller Jamison · Cover design by Saho Fujii · Cover copyright © 2019 by Hachette Book Group, Inc. · Hachette Book Group supports the right to free expression and the value of copyright. The purpose of copyright is to encourage writers and artists to produce the creative works that enrich our culture. · The scanning, uploading, and distribution of this book without permission is a theft of the author's intellectual property. If you would like permission to use material from the book (other than for review purposes), please contact permissions@hbgusa.com. Thank you for your support of the author's rights. · Little, Brown and Company · Hachette Book Group · 1290 Avenue of the Americas, New York, NY 10104 · Visit us at LBYR.com · First Edition: March 2019 · Little, Brown and Company is a division of Hachette Book Group, Inc. · The Little, Brown name and logo are trademarks of Hachette Book Group, Inc. · The publisher is not responsible for websites (or their content) that are not owned by the publisher. · Library of Congress Cataloging-in-Publication Data · Names: Slade, Suzanne. | Miller Jamison, Veronica, illustrator. · Title: A computer called Katherine : how Katherine Johnson helped put America on the moon / written by Suzanne Slade ; Illustrated by Veronica Miller Jamison. · Description: New York : Little, Brown and Company, [2019] | Audience: Age 4–8. · Identifiers: LCCN 2017015316| ISBN 9780316435178 (hardcover) | ISBN 9780316435161 (ebook) | ISBN 9780316470711 (library edition ebook) · Subjects: LCSH: Johnson, Katherine G. | African American women mathematicians—Biography—Juvenile literature. | Women mathematicians—United States—Biography—Juvenile literature. | Mathematicians—United States—Biography—Juvenile literature. · Classification: LCC QA29.J64 S53 2018 | DDC 510.92 [B]—dc23 · LC record available at https://lccn.loc.gov/2017015316 · ISBNs: 978-0-316-43517-8 (hardcover), 978-0-316-51131-5 (ebook), 978-0-316-51132-2 (ebook), 978-0-316-43516-1 (ebook) · PRINTED IN CHINA · APS · 10 9 8 7 6 5 4 3 2 1